HOLLYWOOD

Don Rauf

Created and produced by
Bright Futures Press, Cary, North Carolina
www.brightfuturespress.com

Published by
Cherry Lake Publishing, Ann Arbor, Michigan
www.cherrylakepublishing.com

Photo Credits: cover, Shutterstock/Tischenko Irina; page 5, Shutterstock/Pavel L Photo and Video; page 5, Shutterstock/donatas1205; page 5, Shutterstock/enchanted_fairy; page 7, Shutterstock/ARHIPOV ALEKSEY; page 8, Shutterstock/worldofvector; page 9, Shutterstock/N. Sritawat; page 9, Shutterstock/cobalt88; page 11, Shutterstock/chaoss; page 13, Shutterstock/Africa Studio; page 13, Shutterstock/Oksana Shofrych; page 15, Shutterstock/Bonita R. Chesier; page 17, Shutterstock/Kzenon; page 17, Alex Staroseltsev; page 19, Pavel L Photo and Video; page 21, Shutterstock/Hershel Hoffmeyer; page 21, Shutterstock/Sagittarius Productions; page 23, N Shutterstock/Nejron Photo; page 25, Shutterstock/ Mauricio Graiki; page 25, Shutterstock/ DSBfoto; page 27, Shutterstock/Sorbis; page 29, Shutterstock/James Steidl; page 29, Shutterstock/StockLite.

Library of Congress Cataloging-in-Publication Date

CIP has been filed and is available at catalog.loc.gov.

Printed in the United States of America.

HOLLYWOOD

Lights! Cameras! Action!

You're working in the glitzy world of Hollywood. Hollywood, a community located in sunny southern California, is where most of your favorite television shows and movies are created. It is home to lots of famous (and not so famous) actors and movie directors. It is also home to even more people who work behind the scenes in "show biz." Making TV shows and movies requires what essentially amounts to a small army of professionals. There are people who make costumes, apply makeup, set up lights, control the sound recording, and much more.

In addition to television shows and movies, you also have entertainment-to-go. Thanks to media-streaming services, you can watch your favorite shows on computers or smart phones whenever and wherever you want. All this access means one thing: more original shows are being made. More shows mean more opportunities for show biz professionals!

Whether you want to be in the spotlight or behind it, there are spectacular careers to be found in Hollywood. Pick your favorite path to stardom, and let your Hollywood adventure begin!

TABLE OF CONTENTS

ACTOR

Looking for your big show-biz break? This could be it! Fabulous Films is looking for a fresh new face to star in an action-adventure comedy film about a scary ghost gerbil. Must be able to film on location for three months in the Canadian wilderness. Ability to act with small animals a plus. Send **resume** and head shots to casting **agent**. Difficult divas need not apply.

- *Ready to take on this challenge?*
  Turn to page 6.

- *Want to explore a career as a Camera Operator instead?*
  Go to page 9.

- *Rather consider other choices?*
  Return to page 4.

Explore the performing arts at **http://artsedge. kennedy-center.org/ students**.

You Nailed It!

It's the role that can make you a star! Hundreds of **actors** tried out for the part, but all your hard work and experience paid off—finally!—after so many **auditions**. And so many disappointments. You knew when you came to Hollywood it wouldn't be easy, but you stuck with it, going to audition after audition. Some you nailed, and many you failed. Sometimes the role just wasn't the right fit for you, and that's OK.

Over time you've built a great resume, with appearances in small-budget films. You've learned to memorize lines and how to get so into character that an audience believes you really are that character.

Ready on the Set

Now here you are, on set, filming your first big scene. You can tell this is a quality production. A crew spent weeks building what looks like a room in a haunted house. It is so spooky!

The lighting and sound crew are in position, waiting for the director to shout, "Action!" The makeup artist applies matte and powder to make you look pale and tired. The hairstylist gives your hair a tousled, just-climbed-out-of-bed look. Your costume is rumpled. You look nothing like you! But you do look like a character who's being tormented by a scary ghost gerbil.

Because of your focus, you have your part totally rehearsed. You are also in tip-top shape. Like in many movies, this one requires lots of physical action. In this scene, you are frightened by a ghost, fall out of your chair, and run from the room. You repeat the scene several times in a row because the director does not like the first take…or the second. Sometimes movie directors ask actors to repeat lines dozens of times. Exhausting? Indeed. Glamorous? Not always.

It's a Wrap

You spend several weeks filming **on location**. When you return to Hollywood, there's more work to be done in the studio. It's a great experience, as you've really enjoyed working with the **cast** and crew. It's hard to say good-bye when the director finally says, "It's a wrap!"

You can't wait to see how audiences and critics react when the movie hits the big screen in theaters. Hearing audiences applaud and seeing your name as the credits roll at the end of the film never gets old!

Your Actor Career Adventure Starts Here

EXPLORE IT!

Use your Internet search skills to find out more about these different types of acting roles:

Lead   Co-star

Extra   Supporting role

Stand-in   Cameo

TRY IT!

Memorize a Monologue

Choose a scene from a favorite movie, play, or TV show and write down at least five lines a character says. Memorize them, and perform your monologue for friends.

Role Casting

If you were a casting agent looking for actors to play the following roles in a major movie, which current movie stars (or friends!) would you pick?

- *President of the United States*
- *Super-villain who is a computer genius*
- *Young female scientist, a romantic lead*
- *Middle-age male spy in a romantic comedy*
- *Old professor who moonlights as a wacky inventor*

CAMERA OPERATOR

Television sitcom about a modern family needs camera operator to be the eyes and ears behind the show. Ideal candidate has great visual sense and ability to frame images in a realistic way. Experience with latest and greatest camera equipment required. Team players only! Great gig for tech-savvy entertainment geek. Bring your **portfolio**, and wow us with your artistic skills!

- *Ready to take on this challenge?*
  Turn to page 10.

- *Want to explore a career as a Costume Designer instead?*
  Go to page 13.

- *Rather consider other choices?*
  Return to page 4.

Explore how movies are made at **www. minimoviemakers.com**.

Smile and Say Cheese!

You start out taking selfies with your cell phone and progress to making zany videos starring your friends and family. After a while you're hooked. You go on to pursue a college degree in film school. You get lots of experience working behind the camera, filming sporting events, news segments, and commercials. This is your first shot filming a Hollywood movie, and you are ready!

Keep your eyes on the action. That, in a nutshell, is your main job as a **camera operator**. You see scenes in a way others do not. You know the best angles to get the most out of every scene.

Seen to Be Scene

As the next scene unfolds, you focus your camera. You listen carefully to instructions from the director of photography (also called a **cinematographer**). When the photo director says, "Zoom in," you zoom in and get a clear shot of the lead actor's face. You pan the camera to the right when a co-star comes through the door of the set, and tilt the camera down when that actor takes a seat. When the scene comes to its shocking climax, you zoom in again to get a close-up of the actor's startled reaction. All the fast-paced action keeps on coming, and you have to stay a step ahead. The way you shoot each scene helps tell the story as much as the actor's words.

This is a physical job. Those film cameras are heavy and awkward at first, but you've got the smooth moves! You know not to swing your camera wildly or abruptly. *Just roll with the flow*, you remind yourself.

Practice Makes Perfect

Before each scene, you read over the camera script so you know what to expect. This script gives the order of shots practiced at rehearsal so you can be prepared for each scene. You wear a headset to hear your cues from the director of photography during filming.

The action shots are the most challenging, of course. Sometimes you have to go to great lengths (and heights!) to capture these fast-paced scenes at just the right angle.

This shoot is a breeze because you're comfy with your equipment, and also work well with the director of photography and other camera operators. When you watch the show air on TV, you know you did a good job. Why? Everyone is laughing and enjoying the beautiful scenes you have captured on film...

Your Camera Operator Career Adventure Starts Here

EXPLORE IT!

Use your Internet search skills to find out more about camera operation:

What is the rule of thirds? (Hint: It applies to photography.)

What are "trucking and dollying"? (Hint: It involves camera motions.)

What is a teleprompter? (Hint: It helps when actors forget their lines.)

TRY IT!

Smooth Moves

Next time you are marathon-viewing your favorite show, write down the number of times the camera moves, how it moves, and when the action "cuts" to another camera.

Run Credits

If you watch the credits at the end of a movie or TV show, you will see all the different people involved. Be on the lookout for the following jobs (and look up their definitions if you don't know what they do):

Foley artist	*Gaffer*	*Key grip*
Best boy	*Fix*	*Child wrangler*

COSTUME DESIGNER

TV mini-series needs designer to create historically accurate outfits for Civil War-period piece. Are you known for your good fashion sense? Are you a whiz with a needle, thread, and sewing machine? The perfect candidate is part fashion designer and part historian. Strong research skills essential! Please provide sample sketches.

- *Ready to take on this challenge?*
  Turn to page 14.

- *Want to explore a career as a Director instead?*
  Go to page 17.

- *Rather consider other choices?*
  Return to page 4.

Get a glimpse of the glamorous world of costume design at **http://costumedesignersguild.com.**

Rev Up Your Sewing Machine

Television network representatives were so impressed with your portfolio of designs that they hired you as **costume designer** for a new documentary series. Since you keep all sketches, patterns, and photos of outfits you've created, you were able to show them samples of your best work. All that experience helps seal the deal. It doesn't hurt that you are also a history buff!

Your first step for this period piece on the Civil War is to do your homework. You review books of photographs taken during the Civil War, and make sketches of uniforms and other clothing from the 1800s. You also read the script, so you have a full picture of what's expected. As you sketch out your designs, you get in touch with the film's hairstylist and makeup artist—the outfits you choose are part of a complete look.

Sew Creative

Once you have your designs sketched out, you meet with the movie's director to make sure your designs meet his or her approval. You use your computer to make more detailed images of your creations, and then you meet with actors to take body measurements. You order the right fabrics, buttons, and other sewing supplies to construct the pieces. While you are behind the scenes, your work will be front and center, so it has to be perfect. Plus, with today's high-definition technology, every little detail gets magnified. So you want every stitch and crease perfect.

You have to get a lot of clothing made in a short period of time, so you work with a lot of other seamstresses who are skilled with needle, thread, sewing machines, and following patterns. Don't forget shoes, hats, belts, jewelry, and other style accessories too! They're all important pieces to complete a realistic film.

Final Touches

It's finally the first day of filming. You look out at a set filled with actors who are wearing gray and blue uniforms, as well as women dressed in fancy hoop skirts from that time period. Not bad! If you didn't know otherwise, you might think you'd time-traveled to the Civil War era.

But your work isn't done. Actors' outfits still need adjustments—some are too tight, a strap breaks, and a button pops off. You fix things right away, always at the ready, off camera, sewing needle in hand, as fashion malfunctions spring up.

Carry on, soldier of style!

Your Costume Designer Career Adventure Starts Here

EXPLORE IT!

Find out more online about these elements of fashion design:

Patternmaking

Make-up art

Clothing design software

Hairstyling

TRY IT!

A Cut Above

Conduct an online search for examples of different types of costumes in film or TV that really stand out—from those used in a futuristic **dystopia** like *The Hunger Games* to the swashbuckling garments in *Pirates of the Caribbean.* When you find costumes you like, make sketches of them and add your own special touches to make them uniquely yours.

Transform a Friend

It pays to know how to also do makeup and hair if you're a costume designer. Pick a friend who doesn't mind being your model. Then choose a character you love from a movie or TV show. Doing what you can with makeup and hair, transform your friend into that character. Be sure to take photos and keep them in your portfolio.

DIRECTOR

Are you a natural-born leader? Do you play well with others? Can you juggle many activities at once? OnFleek Films is looking for a hot new director with original style to make short films featuring students in a local high school. Send us your demo reel, and let's get the camera rolling! Academy Award aspirations welcome!

- **Ready to take on this challenge?** Turn to page 18.

- **Want to explore a career as a Special Effects Artist instead?** Go to page 21.

- **Rather consider other choices?** Return to page 4.

Find out more about movie directors at **http://entertainment. howstuffworks.com/ movie-director.htm**.

PRODUCTION
DIRECTOR
SCENE   TAKE   ROLL
DATE

Planning is Everything

OnFleek Films is impressed by your **demo reel**. Your work shows a lot of range and originality so they hire you to direct an intriguing new television series. It's a reality show about what it's like to be a kid in school. Your show features real students in a real school. Expecting the unexpected comes with this job!

As the **director,** you have some planning to do—a phase of the process that's called preproduction. You make plans for how the project's budget is to be spent. You decide on the camera, lights, sound, costumes, and makeup. You pick your student "actors," the stories you want to tell, and choose someone to write the narration. You work with an artist who draws **storyboards** to show the scenes you need to shoot.

Japanese director Akira Kurosawa once said that directing a film is like heading up a military operation—and he was right! You only have two months to film the entire series, so your plan includes a schedule that lists everything you must do to get it all done on time.

Roll Cameras and...Action

You're on the first day of shooting. The scene today is a food fight in a school cafeteria. Your location scout has found the perfect setting and gotten permission to film. You rehearse the actors to make sure they will give you the performance you want. All the actors have their makeup and costumes on. The sound and lighting crew are ready.

You talk with the director of photography (also called the cinematographer) to make sure he is capturing the action just as your picture it. You have specific thoughts about the camera movement and share your ideas to make sure you get the best shots.

Cut!

When you get to the end of filming the food fight scene, you yell, "Cut! That's a wrap."

You and some of your crew review the film clips for any glitches. One of the actors made a mistake saying a line? *Oh, no!* Time for another take. That means a quick cleanup and setting things back exactly as they were. Doing things over is just a normal part of the business, but getting it right is important. You want to capture perfect shots to take into the editing room, where you and the film editor piece together what is sure to be an award-winning film.

Your Director Career Adventure Starts Here

EXPLORE IT!

Find out more about these elements of making a hit movie:

Film editing

Scoring background music

Television producing

Screenplay writing

TRY IT!

Draw It Out!

Directors rely on storyboards to sketch out the sequence of actions. A storyboard is sort of like a comic book version of your film. Pretend you've been hired to make a short film about a kid who loves pizza. Sketch out six to twelve scenes that show how this film would unfold.

Binge Watch!

View a few movies or shows you like, and take notes. Which actors do you like best and why? How is the movie lit? Is the sound effective? What are the camera shots like? Is the story told in an engaging way?

One exercise is to mute the sound as you watch and concentrate on the visuals. Another approach is to listen to the audio of a film with no visuals, and think about the dialog and sound. These exercises can help you better appreciate how a film or TV show is made.

SPECIAL EFFECTS ARTIST

Visual effects studio looking for tech-savvy person to make people fly through the air on brooms, spaceships explode, and dinosaurs come to life. Must-have skills include creativity, attention to detail, and the ability to transform simple scenes into thrilling cinematic experiences. Will work with team to bring dynamic action and imagined worlds to life onto the screen.

- *Ready to take on this challenge?*
  Turn to page 22.

- *Want to explore a career as a Stunt Person instead?*
  Go to page 25.

- *Rather consider other choices?*
  Return to page 4.

Check out some mind-blowing special effects at **www.visualeffectssociety.com.**

Start with a Bang!

The special effects company hires you as a **special effects artist** to work on a new superhero adventure film. The script calls for actors flying through the air, skyscrapers collapsing, and monsters coming to life. You can't wait to get started!

You sit down with the director and screenwriter to go over the scenes you're handling. The scene you begin with is one in which a villain blows up a bridge. You know how to use **computer-generated imagery** (CGI) and combine it with models. So you build a small replica of a bridge, blow it up, and then add special effects with your computer to make it more real. One of your specialties is **pyrotechnics**, or scenes with fire, so you know just what to do to make this scene super scary.

To show actors walking across the bridge as it explodes, you set up a device called a **green screen**. The actors perform these terrifying scenes in front of what is essentially a blank wall. Later on you will insert the film of the exploding bridge behind the actors to make it look like they were on it.

Blood and Guts

Fortunately, the actors survive the blast! But one character gets hit with flying debris and oozes blood from an imaginary head wound. You use a **squib**, a miniature explosive device that ruptures a blood pack, to achieve the full-on gory effect.

Puppet Master

For another scene, you create a realistic half-human/half-lizard monster that battles a superhero on screen. You first build a **maquette**, which is a puppet, or model, of your monster. You scan the maquette to get a full 3-D image in the computer. You even create muscle and bone structure to give the creature realistic, semi-human facial expressions.

You use sophisticated **motion capture** technology that takes images of facial expressions of the human actor who will be the monster. With your computer know-how, you then take images based on your maquette and combine them with the real actor to make a very convincing monster on screen.

You are sitting in the audience when the movie is screened for the first time. When that bridge explodes in the film, the whole audience nearly jumps out of their seats. The audience's startled reactions tell you everything you need to know. Your special effects in the action-adventure movie are a hit! Awesome!

Your Special Effects Artist Career Adventure Starts Here

EXPLORE IT!

Go online to check amazing special effects in these hit films:

Avatar   *Inception*

Jurassic Park   *Ghostbusters*

Star Wars

TRY IT!

Cheap Special Effects

Get inspired by special effects expert, Michael Rosen, as he talks about cool tricks he used to achieve stunning special effects on a budget. Watch it at http://bit.ly/CheapSpecialEffects. Then see what ideas you can mastermind on your own. Use a cell phone or video camera to record the results. Remember, safety first!

The Sound of Special Effects

Sound effects might also be fun to try. Crumbling stiff cellophane paper can sound like a fire. Breaking a handful of spaghetti can sound like breaking a bone. Think of your own sound effects, and try them out. Go online to search for more ideas, using the search term "DIY sound effects" (DIY stands for do-it-yourself!).

STUNT PERSON

Daredevil wanted to jump out of car, fall from the top of building, and fake fistfights in new action film. Athletic candidate in tip-top physical shape preferred. Must have ability to ski, parachute, swim, backflip, climb mountains, do karate, run, and tackle. The more sports skills, the better. Bring experience, and leave fear at home.

- *Ready to take on this challenge?*
  Turn to page 26.

- *Want to explore a career as an Actor instead?*
  Go to page 5.

- *Rather consider other choices?*
  Return to page 4.

Find out what it's like to do stunts in movies at www.stuntmen.com.

Jump On Board

All those daily workouts at the gym are really paying off. Thanks to your most valuable asset—your athletic body—you are in big demand as a Hollywood **stunt person**.

Today you are working as the double for a major movie star. You will spend the day taking the fall—actually, many falls—for that actor. First up is a fight-and-chase scene.

Seeing Double

After a high-protein breakfast, you head over to get your hair and makeup done. While these artists work their magic, you review the storyboards and script. You need to know exactly what is going on in the action scenes you are playing out. Next, you suit up in a costume that matches the lead actor's clothes.

Stunts take a lot of money, time, and effort, so you pay close attention during rehearsal. The whole sequence requires perfect **choreography**. Getting the scene right the first time means fewer takes. Fewer takes mean less wear and tear on your body.

Perfect Execution

The fighting begins! You throw your best "punch" at a "bad guy." The other actor is hooked up to a harness and cable, so when you swing at him, he flies through the air. (The cable is removed from the film digitally in postproduction.)

With the bad guy out cold, you take off on his motorcycle. You see a car speeding toward you and...you jump right over it on your cycle! Timing is everything in scenes like this. One wrong move, and you could be seriously injured. But you've been through this action sequence many times in rehearsals and know just what to do.

Whew! It all goes as planned, and you don't even have a scrape or bruise. Everyone in the cast and crew applauds.

Your work is done—another day, another death-defying feat on film! You grab a healthful smoothie from the food truck and chat with the crew about how awesome it was to watch the live stunt as it happened. When you leave the set, you don't head right home. You grab your longboard and head to the beach for some surfing before the sun goes down. This is what you call mixing business with pleasure!

Your Stunt Person Career Adventure Starts Here

EXPLORE IT!

Go online and find out the meanings of these stunt work terms:

High fall	*Sword fight*
Horsework	*Air ram*
Full body burn	*Car ski*
Descender	*Speed winch*
Wirework	

TRY IT!

Set up Your Own Obstacle Course

Start building your skills as a stunt person by making a fun obstacle course in your backyard or at a park. Give yourself plenty of challenges, and see how fast you can carefully complete it.

Get A Move On

In the world of stunt work, the more athletic you are, the better. Consider looking into martial arts, archery, gymnastics, diving, swimming, horseback riding, wrestling, bicycling, rock climbing, and other sports. Check out ways to get involved at school, or contact your local parks and recreation department for resources. Have fun, and get fit!

WRITE YOUR OWN CAREER ADVENTURE

WRITE YOUR OWN CAREER ADVENTURE

You just read about six awesome Hollywood careers:

- Actor
- Camera operator
- Costume designer

- Director
- Special effects artist
- Stunt person

Which is your favorite? Pick one, and imagine what it would be like to do that job. Now write your own career adventure!

_____

_____

_____

_____

_____

_____

_____

_____

Go online to download free activity sheets at www.cherrylakepublishing.com/activities.

ATTENTION, ADVENTURERS!
Please do NOT write in this book if it is not yours. Use a separate piece of paper.

GLOSSARY

actor person who acts in stage or film productions

agent known as a "talent agent" or "booking agent," a representative who finds jobs for actors, directors, and other professionals in the entertainment business

audition short performance in front of a panel to showcase the talents of a performer

camera operator part of a film crew in a production

cast actors who are in a production

choreography creating and arranging motions, as in dance or action

cinematographer professional in charge of the camera and lighting crews on a film production

computer-generated imagery (CGI) computer graphics used to create special effects and animation in films, television, and video games

costume designer person who designs costumes for a film or stage production

demo reel video or film presentation used to showcase experience for a prospective employer

director person who supervises the actors, camera crew, and other staff for a movie, play, television program, or similar production

dystopia community or society that is undesirable or frightening

green screen background in front of which moving subjects are filmed and which allows a separately filmed background to be added to the final image

on location filming at a place away from the studio

maquette small model of an intended work, used in film to represent a fictional character

motion capture recording of an actor's movements for the purpose of animating a digital character in a movie, TV show, or computer game

pyrotechnics the art of making fireworks

portfolio set of artistic work presented as a collection to represent the range of work an artist can do

resume written summary of professional, educational, and personal qualifications and experience

special effects artist person who creates illusions for movies and television by props, camerawork, and computer graphics

squib small explosive charge that is hidden on an area where a gunshot is to hit

storyboards sequence of drawings showing the scenes planned for a movie or television production

stunt person person who substitutes for an actor in scenes requiring hazardous or acrobatic feats

teleprompter device used in television and moviemaking to project a speaker's script out of sight of the audience

INDEX

ABOUT THE AUTHOR

Don Rauf was the editor-in-chief of *Careers and Colleges* magazine. He has written more than 30 nonfiction books, mostly for children and young adults, including *Killer Lipstick and Other Spy Gadgets*, *The Rise and Fall of the Ottoman Empire*, and *Simple Rules for Card Games*. He lives in Seattle with his wife, Monique, and son, Leo.